Our Father

Padre nostro che sei nei cieli,

sia santificato il tuo nome,

venga il tuo regno,

sia fatta la tua volontà

come in cielo così in terra.

Dacci oggi il nostro pane quotidiano,

e rimetti a noi i nostri debiti

come noi li rimettiamo ai nostri debitori,

e non ci indurre in tentazione,

ma liberaci dal male.

OUR
FATHER

*Reflections on
the Lord's Prayer*

POPE
FRANCIS

A Conversation with Marco Pozza

Translated from the Italian by Matthew Sherry

I

IMAGE
NEW YORK

Copyright © 2017 by Libreria Editrice Vaticana, Citta del Vaticano

Copyright © 2017 by Rizzoli Libri, S.p.A./Rizzoli, Milano

Translation copyright © 2018 by Penguin Random House LLC.

All rights reserved.
Published in the United States by Image, an imprint of the Crown Publishing Group, a division of Penguin Random House LLC, New York.
crownpublishing.com

IMAGE is a registered trademark and the "I" colophon is a trademark of Penguin Random House LLC.

Originally published in Italian by Rizzoli Libri S.p.A. in 2017.

Library of Congress Cataloging-in-Publication Data is available upon request.

ISBN 9780525576112
Ebook ISBN 9780525576129

PRINTED IN THE UNITED STATES OF AMERICA

Jacket design: Sarah Horgan
Front jacket image: Dn Br/Shutterstock

10 9 8 7 6 5 4 3 2 1

First U.S. Edition

"When you pray, do not be like the hypocrites, who love to stand and pray in the synagogues and on street corners so that others may see them. Amen, I say to you, they have received their reward. But when you pray, go to your inner room, close the door, and pray to your Father in secret. And your Father who sees in secret will repay you. In praying, do not babble like the pagans, who think that they will be heard because of their many words. Do not be like them. Your Father knows what you need before you ask him.

This is how you are to pray:

Our Father . . ."

—MATTHEW 6:5–9

Contents

A Note to Readers   9

Preface by Pope Francis: Pray to the Father   11

Our Father   17
  "I Will Not Leave You Orphans"   21

Who Art in Heaven   29
  Fathers and the Our Father   35

Hallowed Be Thy Name   39
  Participating with Prayer in the Work of Salvation   45

Thy Kingdom Come   51
  *The Kingdom of God Needs Our
  Participation*   57

Contents

**Thy Will Be Done on Earth
as It Is in Heaven**   63

Mary's Total "Yes" to the Will of God   67

Give Us This Day Our Daily Bread   73

Feed the Hungry   77

**And Forgive Us Our Trespasses
as We Forgive Those Who
Trespass Against Us**   81

Training for Giving and for Forgiveness   89

And Lead Us Not into Temptation   93

The Foundation of Our Hope   97

But Deliver Us from Evil   101

The Weeds Amid the Good Wheat   105

The Lord's Prayer   111

The Prayer of Grandparents Is a Treasure   117

Afterword by Marco Pozza: An Our Father
Among the Imprisoned   121

Sources   139

A Note to Readers

Teach us to pray.

Image Books is honored to publish *Our Father: Reflections on the Lord's Prayer* on the fifth anniversary of Jorge Mario Bergoglio's election as pope, when he took the name of Francis in honor of Saint Francis, the patron saint of the poor. In this book, a conversation with Fr. Marco Pozza, a priest and prison chaplain from Padua, Italy, the pope offers his heartfelt thoughts on the universal prayer for strength, mercy, and forgiveness.

To mark this special celebration, this book is supplemented with some of Pope Francis's most thoughtful meditations on the Lord's Prayer from throughout his papacy. Certain adjustments in the translation of the original Italian texts, including punctuation and grammar, have been made for the sake of cohesion and consistency.

We hope this book of meditations on the words Jesus used to instruct us on how to pray will bring you comfort, inspiration, and, ultimately, the joy of knowing that our heavenly Father is always with us.

To all, our prayers and blessings.

Gary Jansen, Director of Image Books
March 13, 2018

Pray to the Father

Father.

Without saying this word, without taking it to heart, we cannot pray.

To whom do I pray? Almighty God? Too far away. I cannot feel that he is near. Even Jesus did not refer to God as "the Almighty God."

To whom do I pray? The cosmic God? That is fashionable these days, praying to the cosmic God. But that is nothing but a polytheistic idea of who God is, typified by a lite culture.

To whom do we pray? No, not a cosmic God, but a . . .

Father. We have to pray to the Father! It is a powerful word, "father." We have to pray to the one who has begotten us, the one who has given us life. He has given life to everyone, of course, but "everyone" is too anonymous. He has given life to you. He has given life to me. He is also the one who accompanies us on our journey. He knows our whole lives, the good and the not-so-good. If we do not begin our prayer with this word, spoken not with our lips but with our hearts, we cannot pray as Christians.

We have a Father who is close to us, one who embraces us. All of these anxieties, all of the worries we may have, let us leave them to the Father. He knows what we need.

But wait. How do we understand the word "Father"? Is he my Father? No, he is *our* Father! I am not an only child; none of us is. And if I cannot be a brother, it will be hard for me to truly be a son of this Father, because he is a Father of all. My Father, and that of my brothers and sisters. If I am not at peace with my brothers and sisters, I cannot say "Father" to him.

We cannot pray with enemies in our hearts. This is not easy, I know. Sometimes people will say, "'Father'? I can't say 'Father,' that doesn't work for me." I understand that. Some people have said to me, "I can't say 'our,' because my brother, my enemy, did this or that to me—he should go to hell; he's not family to me!" Acceptance is not easy. But Jesus promised us the Holy Spirit. He is the one who teaches us, from the inside, from the heart, how to say "Father" and how to say "our." Let us then ask the Holy Spirit to teach us to say "Father" and to be able to say "our," thus making peace with our enemies.

This book contains my conversations with Fr. Marco Pozza on the Our Father. Jesus did not give us this prayer simply as a formula for addressing God. With this prayer he is inviting us to turn to the Father so that we can discover who we are and live as his true children and as brothers and sisters together. Jesus shows us what it means to be loved by the Father and reveals to us that the Father wants to pour forth upon us the same love that he has for his Son from all eternity.

So I hope that in saying the Our Father, every one of us will feel ever more loved, forgiven, bathed in the dew of the Holy Spirit, and will thus be able in turn to love and forgive every other brother, every other sister.

This will give us an idea of what heaven is like.

Francis

Our Father

Holy Father, for me the evening of March 13, 2013, the night of your election as pope, was a bit strange. I had turned on the television right after reciting vespers, so according to the Church's liturgy I was already well into March 14, and March 14 is my mom's birthday. On March 13, you came out onto the loggia of the Vatican and we learned with great amazement that you were going to be called Francis, Pope Francis, and my dad's name is Francis. That evening I felt that God was closer to me than ever before. This is why I like to begin by calling you Holy Father. For two reasons: first, because the word "Father" reminds us that we are all children, and then "Holy" because you are a father who proclaims the holiness of God. I would like to start right here, from the concept of "father," because in the prayer that my dad taught me when I was a child, the Our Father, there is almost amazement at seeing a God who would allow his creatures to address him so intimately. I would like to know what it feels like for you to pray the Our Father, to speak to God so intimately.

For me it is reassuring. The Our Father gives me a sense of security: I do not feel uprooted; I do not have the sense of being an orphan. I have a father, a "dad," who brings me a history, shows me how things work, takes care of me, and leads me forward. He

is also a dad before whom I always feel like
a child, because he is great, he is God, and
Jesus asked this of us, to feel like children.
God offers the security of a father, but a
father who accompanies you, waits for you.
Let us think about the parables in chapter
15 of the Gospel of Luke: the lost sheep, the
prodigal son. God is a father who, when you
are sorry about having gone the rotten way,
when you feel bad about a wrong turn you
took and you are rehearsing your speech to
admit your shortcomings, doesn't let you say
it; he embraces you and celebrates. God is a
dad who warns, "Pay attention, look out for
this," he is saying. But he leaves you free to
make your own decision. I think that today
the world has somewhat lost the meaning of
fatherhood. It is a world sick with orphanism.
Saying and taking to heart the Our Father
means understanding that I am not an only
child. It is a risk, that of feeling like only

children, that we Christians run. But no. All. Even those who are outcasts, the outsiders, are children of the same Father. Jesus says to us that it will be the poor, the sinners, the prostitutes, the discarded who enter before you into the kingdom of heaven, all.

I think that if we could do so, many of us would put up a sign in front of God that says "Private Property." God is all mine. This is the temptation. It would be easy to pray to a God who has only one child, and that child is you. Knowing instead that the Father is "ours" may make us feel a bit less alone in difficult times but also in carefree ones.

"I Will Not Leave You Orphans"

One word above all others is dear to us Christians, because it is the name by which Jesus has taught us to call God: "Father." The meaning of this name has received a new depth precisely because of how Jesus used it to speak with God and to manifest his special relationship with him. The blessed mystery of the intimate nature of God—Father, Son, and

Spirit—revealed by Jesus, is the heart of our Christian faith.

"Father" is a word that we all know, a universal word. It indicates a fundamental relationship whose reality is as old as the history of man. Today, however, we have gone so far as to affirm that ours is a "fatherless society." In other words, particularly in Western culture, the figure of the father is seen as being symbolically absent, vanished, removed. At first this absence was perceived as a form of liberation—liberation from the father-master, from the father as representative of a law that is imposed from the outside, from the father as censor of children's happiness and obstacle to the emancipation and autonomy of young adults. At times in the past, authoritarianism, even tyranny in certain cases, held sway in some homes. Some parents often treated their children like slaves, not respecting their need for personal growth. Some fathers did not help their children to set off on their path in freedom (although it is not always easy to bring up a child in freedom). Some fathers did not help their children to take on their responsibilities to build their own future and that of society.

These are certainly not good attitudes; but as often happens, things go from one extreme to the other. The problem in our day no longer seems to be that of the intrusive presence of fathers, but rather of their absence, their desertion. Fathers are sometimes so focused on themselves and their work, and occasionally on their individual fulfillment, that they forget their families. And they leave both younger and older children to themselves.

Back when I was bishop of Buenos Aires, I noticed the sense of orphanhood that young people experience today, and I would often ask dads if they played with their children, if they had the courage and the love to "waste time" with their children. Often the answer was unpleasant: "Well, I can't, because I have so much work. . . ." And the father was absent from that little kid, who was growing up not playing with him, not wasting time with him.

Now I would like to tell all the Christian communities that we must be more mindful of this phenomenon. The absence of the father figure in the lives of children and young adults produces gaps and wounds that can be very grave. And in large degree, the misbehavior of children and adolescents can be attributed to this absence, to the lack of examples and of authoritative guides in their everyday lives, to the lack of closeness, to the lack of love from fathers. It is more profound than we think, the sense of orphanhood that so many young people experience.

There are orphans within families because the dads are often not present in the home, sometimes physically, but sometimes even when fathers are there they do not act like fathers, do not talk with their children, do not fulfill their duty of child-rearing. They do not give their children, through right example accompanied by right words, those principles, those values, those rules of life that they need just as they need bread. The developmental quality of the father's presence is even *more* necessary the more he is required to work and to stay away from home. At times it seems that dads are not sure what place they have in the family, or how to raise their children. And so amid their doubts they hold back; they stand aside and neglect their responsibilities, perhaps taking refuge in an unrealistic

"buddy" relationship with their children.
It is true that you must be your child's
"companion," but do so without forgetting that
you are the father! Acting like nothing more
than a buddy will not be good for your child.

Moreover, we see this problem in the civic
community. The civic community, with its
institutions, has a certain responsibility—we
might call it paternal—toward young people,
a responsibility that it sometimes neglects
or exercises poorly. This too can leave them
orphaned and does not provide them with a
perspective of truth. Young people are thus
left orphaned of sure roads to travel, orphaned
of trustworthy teachers, orphaned of ideals
that would warm their hearts, orphaned of
values and hopes that would sustain them on
a daily basis. They are instead filled with idols,
their hearts stolen away; they are driven to
dream up amusements and pleasures but are

given no jobs; they are duped by the god of money and denied true wealth.

Therefore, it would be good for everyone, for fathers and children, to listen again to the promise that Jesus made to his disciples: "I will not leave you orphans" (Jn 14:18). It is he, in fact, who is the Way to be traveled, the Teacher to be heeded, the Hope that the world can change, that love overcomes hatred, that there can be a future of fraternity and peace for all.

Who Art in Heaven

That localization . . . "in heaven." I am struck on the one hand by the extreme closeness of those who say "Daddy," but at the same time by the distance. I suppose between this closeness and this distance emerge the religions. Perhaps one of the beautiful things about our faith is that it is not man who goes in search of God, but it is God who sets out in search of man. What is meant by "heaven"?

"Heaven" means the greatness of God, his omnipotence. He is the first, he is great, and he is the one who has made us. "Heaven" represents the immensity of his power, of his love, of his beauty. Nevertheless, let us think about the God of Abraham, who draws near to him and says, "I am God Almighty; walk before me, and be blameless" (Gen 17:1). Keep looking up, move forward, believe, hope, and do not give up. God is very close.

However, let us also think about the God who reveals himself on Sinai: "There were thunder and lightning, and a thick cloud upon the mountain, and a very loud trumpet blast" (Ex 19:16). "Mount Sinai was wrapped in smoke, because the Lord descended upon it in fire; and the smoke of it went up like the smoke of a kiln" (Ex 19:18). God reveals himself in glory, in light, in smoke, in cloud; he shows his terrible majesty, and this is something that is hard to understand. You must, I must, we must say "Our Father, who art in heaven," but not with a sense of humiliation. I am reminded of a time when I was five or six years old, and they operated on my throat to take out my tonsils.

At that time, they performed this procedure without anesthesia. The doctor would show you the ice cream you would get afterward, then they put something into your mouth to keep it open, and then the nurse held you. You could not close your mouth. The doctor, then, with a pair of scissors took out both of your tonsils. Moments later, they gave you the ice cream and that was it.

After the operation, I could not speak because of the pain, and my dad called a taxi and we went home. Once we arrived at home, Dad paid the driver and I was shocked: *Why does*

Dad pay this man? As soon as I was able to talk, two days later, I asked him, "Why did you pay that man with the car?" He explained to me that it was a taxi. "But wait, wasn't the car yours?" I asked him. You see, at the time, I thought my dad owned all the cars in the city!

The memory of this childhood experience with a father who teaches and explains, especially when we are experiencing pain, gives us an idea of our relationship with God, his greatness but also his closeness. God is a God of glory, but he walks with you and when it is necessary, he even gives you ice cream.

Let us revisit the idea of "orphanhood." I have a friend who said to me once, "I'm not interested in knowing if something like a father truly exists; if he does that's his problem." Another time I asked someone in prison (one of my parishioners, since my parish is the prison), "Why did you leave home

when you were young?" He said to me, "Because
it was impossible to breathe when my father was
around." Yet both of them, when they discovered
that their fathers were dying, returned to their
bedside to say goodbye. Perhaps it is a sort of
modern-day version of the parable in chapter 15 of
Luke: We go home not because we are hungry but
because we know a father is waiting there for us.

Yes, he is always there waiting for us. And
"in heaven" he is powerful and great and
majestic—this is what the expression "who art
in heaven" means—but he is close and walks
with us.

Fathers and the Our Father

The first thing needed is this: that the father be present in the family. That he be close to his wife, to share everything, joys and sorrows, hardships and hopes. A father needs to be close to the children as they grow up; when they are playing and when they are working on a task; when they are carefree and when they are troubled. He needs to be there when they are outgoing and when they are withdrawn; when they are daring and when they are fearful; when they make a misstep and when they get back on track; the father must be present, always. Being present does not mean being in control! Because fathers who control too much are crushing their children, they are not letting them grow up.

The Gospel speaks to us of the exemplary nature of the Father who is in heaven—the only one, Jesus says, who can truly be called "good Father" (cf. Mk 10:18). We have already mentioned the parable of "the prodigal son," or better, of "the merciful father," which is found in the Gospel of Luke, chapter 15 (cf. 15:11–32). What dignity and tenderness there is in how the father stands at the door of that house, waiting for his son to come back! Fathers have to be patient. So many times there is nothing that can be done but wait with patience, kindness, generosity, and mercy, and pray.

A good father knows how to wait and knows how to forgive sincerely. Of course, he also knows how to give firm correction. He is not a weak father, a pushover, sentimental. The father who knows how to correct without discouraging is the same one who knows how to protect without sparing himself. One time at a conference on the topic of marriage, I heard one dad say, "Sometimes I have to discipline my kids a little, but I never humiliate them." How beautiful! The father has a sense of dignity. He has to reprimand, but he does it in the right way, to correct behavior, and then moves on.

Therefore, if there is someone who can fully explain the prayer of the Our Father as taught

by Jesus, it is precisely someone with his own
personal experience of fatherhood. Without
the grace that comes from the Father who is in
heaven, fathers lose courage and abandon the
field. However, children need to find a father
who is waiting for them when they return
from their failures. These children will do all
they can in order not to admit their mistakes,
not to let their embarrassment show, but they
need this security. Not finding their father at
the door opens wounds inside of them that are
difficult to heal.

The Church, our mother, is committed to
supporting with all her strength the good
and generous presence of fathers in families.
For the younger generations, fathers are the
irreplaceable guardians and mediators of faith
in the goodness, of faith in the justice, and faith
in the protection of God, like Saint Joseph.

Hallowed Be
Thy Name

The prayer of the Our Father continues in a way that may seem a little odd. It says, "hallowed be thy name." When I hear the word "name," I am reminded of a saying from my hometown: "Hold on to your good name." In other words, take care of your reputation. How does a pope translate the hallowing of God's name, which in itself is already holy? Has someone perhaps taken this holiness,

*profaned it, and are we asking God to cleanse it
again with his grace?*

"Hallowed be thy name" means it should be
hallowed, it should be revered and honored, in
us, in me. Because many times we believers,
we Christians, present a testimony that is
sad, ugly. We say that we are Christians; we
say that we have a father, but we live like—I
do not want to say like animals, but we often
live like people who do not believe either in
God or in man. We live without faith; we
live not in love but in hatred, in competition,
in war; we live in doing evil. Is God's name
therefore hallowed in Christians who fight
among themselves for power? Is it hallowed in
the lives of those who pay a hit man to get rid
of an enemy as we see happen in Rome and
around the world? No, there God's name is
not hallowed. It has been forsaken.

An experience that I sometimes have in my prison parish reminds me of your preaching. I know a prisoner who falls asleep every time he comes to church. I tried to tell him once, "Look, maybe it's not a good habit to sleep in church." He gave me a wonderful answer: "You know, I am sick in the head, I can't get to sleep anywhere, and the only time my thoughts leave me alone is when I am in church." It made me think of how one day, when a young man confessed to you, "I sometimes fall asleep when I am at adoration," you replied, "It doesn't matter. God keeps looking at you." This prisoner teaches me what it means to hallow the name, how to do adoration.

Letting God look at us, letting God adore us. I too, when I go to pray, sometimes fall asleep, and Saint Thérèse of the Child Jesus said that it happened to her too, and the Lord, God, the Father likes it when someone falls asleep. Psalm 130 (or 131, depending on the numbering) says, "I have calmed and quieted my soul, like a child quieted at its mother's breast; like a child that is quieted is my soul." This is one of the many ways to hallow God's name: to feel like a child in his hands.

God's name is mercy. . . .

It is mercy. This is true. God forgives everything; he forgives everything. One time the image of Our Lady of Fatima came to Buenos Aires and there was a Mass for the sick in a big stadium full of people. I was already a bishop then, and I went to hear confessions. I heard confessions before the Mass and after it. Finally, there was practically no one left and I got up to leave, because I had to go somewhere else for a confirmation. But a little woman came up to me—simple, dressed in black like the rural women of southern Italy when they are in mourning. Her splendid eyes

lit up her face. "You want to go to confession,"
I said to her, "but you don't have any sins."
The lady was Portuguese, and she answered
me, "All of us have sinned." I teased her,
"Be careful, then: perhaps God does not
forgive." "God forgives everything," she said
confidently. "And how do you know that?" I
asked. "If God did not forgive everything,"
she answered, "the world would not exist." I
wanted to ask her, "Have you studied at the
Gregorian University?"

It is the wisdom of the simple who know
they have a father who is always waiting for
them. God is not waiting for you to knock
at his door; it is he who knocks at yours,
unsettling your heart. He is waiting for
you first. I like to say it in Spanish: *Dios
nos primerea.*

He makes the first move.

God makes the first move. This is mercy.

One priest of my diocese gave this interpretation of mercy while speaking in prison: "Jesus says to us, 'Have you messed up? It doesn't matter; I'll pay for it.'" How wonderful, this God who acts in advance, this God who acts on our behalf.

Participating with Prayer in the Work of Salvation

In the Gospel of Luke, chapter 11, Jesus prays alone, off by himself. When he is finished, the disciples ask him, "Lord, teach us to pray" (v. 1); and he replies, "When you pray, say: 'Father . . .'" (v. 2). This word is the "secret" of the prayer of Jesus; it is the key that he himself gives us so that we too may enter into that relationship of confidential dialogue with the

Father, which accompanied and sustained his whole life.

There are two requests that Jesus associates with the title Father: "hallowed be thy name" and "Thy kingdom come" (v. 2). The prayer of Jesus, and therefore Christian prayer, is first a matter of making room for God, allowing him to manifest his holiness in us, and also advancing his kingdom through the possibility of exercising his lordship of love in our lives.

Three more requests complete this prayer that Jesus teaches, the Our Father. They are three petitions that express our fundamental needs: bread, forgiveness, and help in temptation (cf. vv. 3–4). The bread that Jesus has us ask for is that which is necessary, not the superfluous; it is the bread of the pilgrim, just enough, a bread that is not hoarded and not wasted, that does not slow us down on our way. The forgiveness is, first, that which we ourselves receive from God. Only the awareness that we are sinners forgiven by the infinite divine mercy can make us capable of carrying out concrete actions of fraternal reconciliation. If a person does not feel like a forgiven sinner, he will never be able to perform an act of forgiveness or reconciliation. It begins from the heart, where we feel like forgiven sinners. The last request, "lead us not into temptation," expresses the awareness of our condition, which is one of constant exposure to the snares of evil and corruption. All of us know what temptation is!

The teaching of Jesus on prayer continues with two parables, in which he takes as a model the attitude of one friend toward another and of a father toward his son (cf. vv. 5–12). Both of them are intended to teach us to have complete trust in God, who is Father. He knows our needs better than we ourselves do, but he wants us to present them to him with boldness and insistence, because this is our way of participating in his work of salvation. Prayer is the first and primary "tool" in our hands! Insisting with God does not serve to convince him, but to strengthen our faith and our patience, which means our ability to fight along with God for the things that are truly important and necessary. There are two of us in prayer: God and me, fighting together for the important things.

One of these is the great important thing that Jesus says in the Gospel but for which we almost never ask, and that is the Holy Spirit. "Give me the Holy Spirit!" And Jesus says this: "If you then, who are evil, know how to give good gifts to your children, how much more will the heavenly Father give the Holy Spirit to those who ask him!" (Lk 11:13). The

Holy Spirit! We have to ask that the Holy Spirit come to us. But how does the Holy Spirit help us? He helps us to live well, to live with wisdom and love, doing God's will. What a wonderful prayer it would be, this week, for every one of us to pray, "Father, give me the Holy Spirit!" Our Lady the Virgin Mary shows us how with her life, completely enlivened by the Spirit of God. May she help us to pray to the Father in union with Jesus, that we may live, not in a worldly manner but according to the Gospel, guided by the Holy Spirit.

Thy Kingdom Come

*Then there is that third line: "thy kingdom come."
Jesus has already come; the incarnation has taken
place, back in Bethlehem, the great amazement of
humanity. Still today, however, it almost seems
that I can hear the echoes of that wonderful song,
that invocation the bride makes to the bridegroom,
"Maranatha—come, Lord Jesus." Many times in
the Gospel it says, "The kingdom of God is here."
There is an urgency, "Convert, believe in the*

Gospel!" But in the Our Father, it almost seems that the tense changes to "may it come," a plea aimed at the future. I know that it will come, eventually, but then curiosity seizes me: How is it possible to see the kingdom of God being born?

The kingdom of God is here *and* the kingdom of God will come. It is the treasure hidden in the field; it is the precious pearl for the sake of which the merchant sells all he has (cf. Mt 13:44–46). The kingdom of God is the good wheat that grows alongside the weeds, and you have to fight against the weeds (cf. Mt 13:24, 40). The kingdom of God is also hope; the kingdom of God is coming now but at the same time has not yet come completely. This is how the kingdom of God has already come: Jesus has taken flesh, he has become man like us, he walks with us, and he gives us hope for our tomorrow: "I am with you always, to the close of the age" (Mt 28:20).

The kingdom of God is something that belongs to us, or rather, it is better to think of it another way: we must allow ourselves to be possessed by the certainty that it has come. This is true Christian faith. But at the same time there is also the need to cast the anchor there and to hold on to the cord because the Kingdom is still coming. We do not possess the rope fully, and there is always the risk that it will slip from our hands. This is true Christian hope. These two actions are very important: faith and hope.

The two times of salvation: the already and the not-yet. I would not want to twist the meaning of the Gospel, but there is an image that I relate to the kingdom of God: My dad, when I was little, told me the story of Fr. Lorenzo Milani, and I know that a little while ago you were in Barbiana, outside Florence. For me Barbiana is a little piece of the kingdom of God. That's how

I imagine heaven. When I see the poor taking charge of their story I think that the kingdom of God is emerging there, in Barbiana, in Bozzolo, in prisons, perhaps even at my house, sometimes. Am I wrong?

No, you are not wrong. In Barbiana, I was struck by a sense of "I care," which goes against the "it doesn't matter to me" attitude of the fascist era. There is a sense of responsibility there. It is needed everywhere. I am reminded of an expression: "The protagonist of history is the beggar." Perhaps Péguy said it. History is made by those who are the most poor. They are the protagonists of salvation. Jesus is with them, and with everyone. But that invitation to the banquet in the Bible for the son who was getting married says, "Let everyone come, good and bad, all." God's preference is nonetheless for the poor. The protagonist of history is the beggar, but

not only the material beggar but ourselves too,
spiritual beggars. May your kingdom come,
Lord, because without you we can do nothing.

To say "thy kingdom come" is to be a beggar.

Beautiful! The kingdom of the beggar.

The Kingdom of God Needs Our Participation

Two brief parables help us to understand God's Kingdom better, that of the seed that sprouts and grows by itself, and that of the mustard seed (cf. Mk 4:26–34). Through these images taken from the rural world, Jesus presents the efficacy of the Word of God and the demands of his kingdom, demonstrating the reasons for our hope and our effort in history.

The first parable focuses on the fact that
the seed, cast upon the ground, *takes root
and develops on its own*, whether the farmer
is asleep or awake. In the language of the
Gospel, the seed is the symbol of the Word of
God, the fecundity of creation. As the humble
seed develops in the ground, so the Word
operates with the power of God in the heart
of the one who listens to it. God has entrusted
his Word to our ground, meaning to each
one of us with our concrete humanity. We
can be confident because the Word of God is
a creative word, destined to become "the full
grain in the ear" (v. 28). This Word, if it is
accepted, certainly bears its fruit, because God
himself makes it sprout and ripen by means
that we cannot always evaluate and in a way
that we do not know (cf. v. 27). All of this
helps us understand that it is always God, it
is always God who makes his kingdom grow.
This is why we pray so much, "thy kingdom

come." It is he who makes it grow; man is his humble assistant who contemplates and rejoices in the divine creative action and patiently waits for its fruit.

The Word of God brings growth, it gives life. And here I would like to remind us once again about the importance of having the Gospel, the Bible, near at hand—a little Gospel in the purse, in the pocket—and of nourishing ourselves every day with this living Word of God, to read every day a passage of the Gospel, a passage of the Bible. Never forget this, please. This action makes the life of God's kingdom sprout within us.

The second parable uses the image of the mustard seed. Despite being the *smallest* of all the seeds, it is full of life and grows until it becomes "the *greatest* of all shrubs" (Mk 4:32). This is what the kingdom of

God is like, a reality that in human terms is small and apparently irrelevant. In order to appreciate it one must be poor in heart, not trust in one's own capabilities, behave in ways as to be unimportant in the eyes of the world but precious in the eyes of God, who favors the simple and the humble. When we live like this, the power of Christ bursts through us and transforms that which is small and modest into a reality that leavens the entire dough of the world and of history.

These two parables convey an important teaching: the kingdom of God needs *our participation*, but it is above all an *initiative and gift of the Lord*. Our feeble work may appear small in the face of the complexity of the world's problems, but if embedded within God's work it has no fear of the difficulties. The Lord's victory is assured: *his love will cause to sprout and grow every seed of goodness present*

on the earth. This opens us up to trust and
hope, in spite of the tragedy, the injustice, the
suffering that we encounter. The seed of justice
and peace sprouts and develops because it is
ripened by the merciful love of God.

May the Holy Virgin, who like "fertile
ground" received the seed of the divine Word,
sustain us in this hope that never fails us.

Thy Will Be Done on Earth as It Is in Heaven

The invocation "thy kingdom come" connects very readily with "thy will be done." I confess, Pope Francis, that at times as a priest I still get a bit confused between my will and the will of God. I am like Lady Prassede in The Betrothed. *She is mixed up between the divine and her own brain, and then says, "I have done the will of heaven." Perhaps there is an echo of what the world says today: "There you have it: the usual passivity of*

Christians; they accept everything that comes."
In reality, I would dare say that doing the will of
God is almost the opposite. It means making room
for a God who permeates us, who draws us to
himself.

Let us take the Ten Commandments that
God revealed to his people at the beginning
of the pilgrimage to the Promised Land.
They represent the core of God's will, and it
is curious that only three of them have to do
directly with him: the will of God is not to
steal, not to kill, not to do evil, not to be a
liar. . . . Truth means proceeding on a path
that becomes wider the more its meaning is
explored. It becomes wider, and at the same
time more subtle through the delicacy of the
soul. It's in the little acts of God's will, the
little acts. If we are sincere and open with the
Lord, we will be able to do God's will, because
God does not conceal his will; he makes it

known to those who seek it. He does not force those who are not interested in his will, but he is waiting for them. He is always waiting.

God's will is that ultimately nothing be lost.

That nothing be lost.

He is a God in waiting. I know that you love Jorge Luis Borges, who wrote: "In the cracks is God, who lies in wait."

Yes, ours is precisely a God in waiting. That is why when he realizes that someone is lost, he leaves those who are not lost and goes in search of the wayward.

Mary's Total "Yes" to the Will of God

I want to focus on two passages in the Bible that relate to the Blessed Virgin Mary. They present two crucial insights into the history of relations between man and God. We could say that they lead us to the origin of good and evil.

The book of Genesis shows us the first "no," the original "no," the human "no," when man preferred to look to himself instead of to his Creator, when he wanted to do things his own way and chose to be self-sufficient. But in doing this, in leaving his communion with God, he lost his very self and began to be afraid, to hide and to accuse the one near him (cf. Gen 3:10, 12). These are the symptoms: fear is always a symptom of a "no" to God; it indicates that I am saying "no" to God; accusing others and not looking at myself indicates that I am distancing myself from God. This is what sin does. However, the Lord does not leave man at the mercy of his own evil; he immediately seeks him out and asks him a question that is full of apprehension: "Where are you?" (v. 9). As if to say, "Stop, think. Where are you?" It is the question of a father or mother who is looking for the lost child: "Where are you? In what situation have you ended up?" And this God does with so much patience, to the point of bridging the distance caused by the Fall.

A second crucial passage in the Gospels is when God comes to dwell among us, becomes man like us. And this was made possible by a great "yes"—that of Mary at the moment of the Annunciation. Through this "yes" Jesus began his journey on the paths of humanity; he began it in Mary, spending the first months of his life in his mama's womb. He did not appear as a full-grown adult but followed the whole path of a human being. He became like us in all things, except for one: sin, that "no." This is why he chose Mary, the only creature without sin, immaculate. In the Gospel, with just one word, she is called "full of grace" (Lk 1:28), meaning filled by grace. It means that in her, filled by grace from the very first, there is no room for sin. And we too, when we turn to her, recognize this beauty. We invoke her as "full of grace," without a shadow of evil.

Mary responds to God's proposal, saying, "Behold, I am the handmaid of the Lord" (v. 38). She does not say, "Well, this time I'll do God's will, I'll go along with it, then I'll see. . . ." No. Hers is a "yes" that is full, total, for life, unconditional. And just as the original "no" had closed man's passage to God, so Mary's "yes" opened the pathway to God among us. It is the most important "yes" in history, the humble "yes" that overturns the arrogant "no" at the beginning, the faithful "yes" that heals the disobedience, the accommodating "yes" that reverses the selfishness of sin.

For us as well there is a salvation history made of yeses and nos. At times, however, we

are experts in the "half yes." We are great at
pretending that we do not really understand
what God wants and what conscience suggests
to us. We even get crafty about it, and in
order to avoid actually saying "no" to God
we say, "Excuse me, I can't," "Not today,
maybe tomorrow," "Tomorrow I'll be better,
tomorrow I'll pray, I'll do good, tomorrow."
These attitudes and decisions distance us from
the "yes." They distance us from God and lead
us to the "no," to the "no" of sin, to the "no" of
mediocrity.

All of this leads to closing the door on
goodness. Evil takes advantage of the
withheld "yes." Each one of us has a collection
of these inside. If we think about it, we will
find many of these withheld yeses. Instead,
every full "yes" to God gives rise to a new
history. Sin makes us old inside. It ages us fast!
But saying "yes" to God is literally original.

Every "yes" to God originates histories of salvation for us and for others. Like Mary, with her "yes."

God wants to visit us and is waiting for our "yes." Let us keep in mind what "yes" we should say to God today. It will do us good to think and live this way. We will find within us the voice of the Lord, who is asking us for something, a step forward. We all need to say, "I believe in you, I hope in you, I love you; may your will for good be fulfilled in me." This is the "yes." With generosity and trust, like Mary, let us say today, each one of us, say "yes" to God.

Give Us This Day Our Daily Bread

Now comes the opening of the second part of the Lord's Prayer. While the first invocations were made in God's name, now we are asking for something for ourselves. We have thought of the one who loves us; now the hope is that he may think of us and "Give us this day our daily bread." I am fascinated by that plural, "give us," since God is "our" Father. I believe that God is thinking about me today, on this very day.

All of this, in the kingdom of God as recounted to us in the Gospel, happens while we are seated at table. Jesus uses this image often. The kingdom of God is always a celebration; we are at table, so he gives us something to eat. Whether it is a special occasion or an everyday meal, we are at table. The power of God's presence in the world today is precisely at table, in the Eucharist with Jesus. This is why we ask that he feed all of us. Feed us with that spiritual food that strengthens us, at table in the Eucharist, but also feed everyone, in this world in which the reign of hunger is so cruel. When we pray the Our Father, it would be good for us to linger a bit over this petition—"give us bread today," to me and to all—and to think about how many people do not have this bread. At home as children, when a piece of bread fell, my family taught us to pick it up right away and kiss it. Bread was never thrown away. Bread is a symbol of the unity of humanity; it is a symbol of God's love for you, the God who feeds you. When it gets stale, what do moms and grandmas do with the bread? They soak it in milk, make it into a cake, they do something with it. Bread is never thrown away.

My grandma, when my brother and I would shoot bread pellets at each other, would say: "Children, we don't play with bread." Now when I lift up the Eucharist as a priest, I hear inside me the words of my grandma. With this bread too, above all with this bread, there must be no playing around. For a Christian, bread is the Eucharist.

But bread is the *other* as well! Let us not forget the work of mercy that urges us to feed the hungry.

In prison, I sometimes imagine the Eucharist less as a reward than as a medicine. If I mess up, I need God not to take his bread away from me but to make me feel that I am his child.

That is exactly right. As I wrote in *Evangelii Gaudium*, the Eucharist "is not a prize for the perfect but a powerful medicine and nourishment for the weak."

Yes, it lets me know that I am in God's heart, even if I have fallen.

Feed the Hungry

In the Bible, one of the Psalms says that God is the one who "gives food to all flesh" (136:25). The experience of hunger is harsh. Those who have gone through periods of war or famine know it. Yet this experience is repeated every day and lives side by side with abundance and waste. The words of the apostle James are always timely: "What does it profit, my brethren, if a man says he has faith but has not works? Can his faith save him? If a brother or sister is ill clad and in lack of daily food, and one of you says to them, 'Go in peace, be warmed and filled,' without giving them the things needed for the body, what does it profit? So faith by itself, if it has no works, is dead," because it is incapable of doing works, of doing charity, of loving. Always someone is hungry and thirsty and needs me. I cannot delegate this to anyone else. This poor person needs me, my help, my words, my efforts. We are all in this together.

This is also the teaching of the Gospel in which Jesus, seeing the many people who have been following him for hours, asks his disciples, "How are we to buy bread, so that these people may eat?" (Jn 6:5). And the disciples respond, "It is impossible, it would be better for you to send them away. . . ." Instead, Jesus says, "You give them something to eat"

(Mk 6:37). Jesus has them give him the few loaves and fish that they have with them, blesses them, breaks them, and has them distributed to all. This is a very important lesson for us. It tells us that the little we have, if we entrust it to the hands of Jesus and share it with faith, becomes an overflowing treasure.

Pope Benedict XVI, in the encyclical *Caritas in Veritate*, affirms, "*Feed the hungry* is an ethical imperative for the universal Church. . . . The right to food, like the right to water, has an important place within the pursuit of other rights. . . . It is therefore necessary to cultivate a public conscience that considers food and access to water as universal rights of all human beings, without distinction or discrimination" (no. 27). Let us not forget the words of Jesus: "I am the bread of life" (Jn 6:35) and "If any one thirst let him come to me and drink" (Jn 7:37). These words are

a challenge for all of us believers, a challenge
to recognize that feeding the hungry and
giving drink to the thirsty are a conduit of
our relationship with God, a God who has
revealed in Jesus his face of mercy.

And Forgive Us Our Trespasses as We Forgive Those Who Trespass Against Us

Next we have this beautiful image: "Forgive us our trespasses as we forgive those who trespass against us." Here I am reminded of one of my prisoners, who on Christmas Eve last year was reading the prayer of the faithful, and it said, "Let us pray to God our savior." He made a little mistake and said, "Let us pray to God our solderer," and I flashed back to an image of my dad with a soldering iron. There are two broken pieces; Dad does not throw them away but repairs them with the soldering iron. I thought to myself, Leave it to the poor to translate the mercy of God for me. What remains unresolved for me is the question of the adverb "as." Does it mean, "so that we too may do this" or "to the extent to which I forgive, may you also forgive me, Lord"?

It is a petition that the bankers like! The original Latin expression says, "Forgive us our debts"; that is why bankers like this petition. They like the first part, in which they are forgiven. They do not like to forgive others; they do not forgive debts in this world, where at the center of everything is money. Forgiveness, forgiveness. It is so difficult to forgive. There is just one condition, however, without which no one can ever forgive. You will be able to forgive if you have had the grace of feeling forgiven. Only the person who feels forgiven is capable of forgiving. I forgive because, first, I have been forgiven. Think instead of the doctors of the law, the Pharisees, those who made war on Jesus. They believed they were the righteous. They did not need forgiveness and did not understand why Jesus forgave sinners, ate with them, healed them, and associated with the leprous. Jesus forgave everyone, and the Pharisees did not understand, because they felt so righteous that they could not savor that wonderful experience. I too will recount, as a Christian, as a person, what I have experienced. Once, when I felt that the Lord had forgiven me of so many things, I wept with joy. Still today, when I think back on how I wept and it is my turn to forgive, I say to myself, "There's no comparison; this is a small thing compared with the time God showed you great mercy."

*I will confide something to you, Pope Francis. I
used to be one of those who think that people who
mess up should be marched off to prison. Now
God is giving me the grace to be a pastor to these
people, together with them. I too remember the
day, the hour, of this encounter. Since that day, my
life has never been the same. In being ashamed,
I felt the stirrings of rebirth. I learned this in
reading one of your texts, on the grace of being
able to experience shame. I was ashamed because
I had driven God out of my life and found myself
returning to the road of seeking the Father. There
is nothing I guard more jealously in my heart
than having looked at myself in the mirror and
experiencing immense shame at having distanced
myself from him. From our home.*

In the account of Jesus's Passion, three
episodes speak to us of shame. Three persons
who become ashamed. The first is Peter. Peter
hears the cock crow, and in that moment, he

feels something inside himself and sees Jesus come out and look at him. The shame is such that he weeps bitterly (cf. Lk 22:54–62). The second case is that of the good thief. "We are here," he says to his companion in misfortune, "because we have done wicked and unjust things, but this poor innocent man has done nothing wrong. . . ." He feels guilty, he is ashamed, and Saint Augustine says that in this way he gained paradise (cf. Lk 23:39–43). The third, the one that moves me the most, is the shame of Judas. Judas is a figure who is difficult to understand, though there have been many interpretations of his personality. In the end, however, when he sees what he has done, he goes to the "righteous," to the priests, and says, "I have sinned, because I have betrayed innocent blood." They reply to him, "What does that have to do with us? See to it yourself" (cf. Mt 27:3–10). So he goes off with the guilt that suffocates him. Perhaps if he had found Our Lady, things would have changed, but the poor guy goes away, finds no way out, and hangs himself. However, there is one thing that makes me think that the story of Judas does not end there. Maybe someone will think, "This pope is a heretic." Not at all! Go look at a specific medieval capital or column in the Basilica of Saint Mary Magdalene in Vézelay, in Burgundy. The men of the Middle Ages did catechesis through architecture, sculptures, images. On one side of the capital is Judas after he hanged himself, but on the other is the Good Shepherd lifting him onto his shoulders and taking him with him. On the lips of the Good Shepherd is the hint of a smile that I would not call ironic, but somewhat shrewdly knowing. Behind my desk, I keep a photograph of this capital divided into two sections, because it helps me meditate. There are many ways to be ashamed; despair is one of them, but we must try to help the desperate so that they may find the true path of shame, and not travel the one that ends with Judas. These three figures of Jesus's Passion help me so much. Shame is a grace. Where I am from in Argentina, a person who does not know how to behave and does wrong is called "shameless."

Training for Giving and for Forgiveness

The family is a big training gym for the mutual giving and forgiveness without which no love can last for long. Without giving of oneself and without forgiving one another, love does not last; it does not endure. In the prayer that he himself has taught us—the Our Father—Jesus has us ask the Father, "Forgive us our trespasses, as we forgive those who trespass against us." And in the end he comments: "For if you forgive men their trespasses, your heavenly Father also will forgive you; but if you do not forgive men their trespasses, neither will your Father forgive your trespasses" (Mt 6:14–15). One cannot live without forgiveness—or at least, one cannot live well, especially in the family. Every day we do wrong to one another. We have to take stock of these mistakes, due to our frailty and our selfishness. But what is asked of us is to heal right away the wounds that we cause, to repair immediately the threads that we break in the family. If we wait too long it becomes too difficult. And there is a simple secret for healing wounds and dispelling accusations. It is this: do not let the day end without apologizing, without making peace between husband and wife, between parents and children, between brothers and sisters . . . between daughter-in-law and mother-in-law! If we learn to apologize right away and to forgive one another, then wounds heal, marriage becomes stronger, and the family becomes an ever more solid house, one that withstands the impacts of our wrongdoings large and small. And this is why there is no need to make a big speech. A caress is enough. One caress and everything is over; it is time to move on. But never end the day at war!

If we learn to live like this in the family, we will do the same outside of it, wherever we find ourselves. It is easy to be skeptical about this. Many—even among Christians—think that this is an exaggeration. "Yes," they say, "those are beautiful words, but it is impossible to put them into practice." But thanks to God, that is not the case. In fact, it is precisely in receiving forgiveness from God that we in turn are capable of forgiving others. This is why Jesus has us repeat these words every time we recite the prayer of the Our Father, every day. And it is indispensable that, in a society that is merciless at times, there should be places, like the family, where we can learn to forgive one another.

And Lead Us Not into Temptation

Despair is a temptation. And so we come to the second to last invocation, "lead us not into temptation." I have friends, some believers and some not, who ask me every now and then, "Father Marco, can God lead us into temptation?" I like to interpret the invocation this way: "Since Satan is tempting me, help me not to fall into the snare of his seductions." I cannot believe that God would tempt me.

This, "lead us not into temptation," is not a good translation. In fact, if we open the Gospel in the latest edition of the Italian episcopal conference, we read, "do not abandon us to temptation" (Lk 11:4; Mt 6:13). The French have also changed the text, with a translation that means "Do not let me fall into temptation." *I am the one who falls.* It is not God who tosses me into temptation in order to see how I fall. A father does not do this. A father helps his child get up right away. The one who leads us into temptation is Satan. That is Satan's craft. The meaning of our prayer is, "When Satan leads me into temptation, please God, give me a hand, give me your hand." It is like that painting in which Jesus holds his hand out to Peter, who is imploring him, "Lord, save me, I am drowning, give me your hand!" (cf. Mt 14:30).

*In our prison parish the biggest temptation
with which Satan tries to seduce the heart
every morning is to whisper, "Give up. Your
imprisonment doesn't change anything; it's all a
waste of time." To despair, for me, means to stop
looking at the face of Christ.*

Jesus is the hope, the anchor.

*It is also true, however, that when I am tempted
I realize how much grace God has given me in my
heart. Perhaps I would not have become aware of
this if I had not been tempted. Where I come from,
they always say that no one can boast of being
chaste if he has never been tempted.*

This is true. That is a good expression.

The Foundation of Our Hope

Let us go back and meditate on the parable of the merciful father (cf. Lk 15:11–32). Jesus tells the story of a father who knows only how to be love for his children. A father who does not punish his son for his arrogance, and is even capable of giving him his portion of the inheritance and letting him leave home. God is Father, Jesus says, but not in the human way, because there is no father in this world who would act like the one in this parable. God is Father in his own way: good, unguarded in the face of human free will, capable only of conjugating the verb "to love." When the rebellious son, after squandering everything, finally comes back home, that father does not apply criteria of human justice, but first of all feels the need to forgive, and with his embrace makes his son understand that the whole long time he was missed, sorely missed by his loving father.

What an unfathomable mystery is a God who harbors this kind of love for his children!

Perhaps this is why, in evoking the heart of the Christian mystery, the apostle Paul does not even try to translate into Greek a word that Jesus, in Aramaic, pronounced as *Abbà*. There are two places in his letters (cf. Rm 8:15; Gal 4:6) where Saint Paul touches upon this theme, and in both places he leaves that word untranslated, in the same form in which it blossomed on the lips of Jesus, *Abbà*—a term even more intimate than "father," and one that some translate as "Papa," "Daddy."

We must remember we are never alone. Some of us may be far away from God, hostile; we may even claim to be "godless." But the Gospel of Jesus Christ reveals to us that God cannot be without us. He will never be a "manless" God. It is he who cannot be without us, and this is a great mystery! God cannot be God without man. What a great mystery this is! And this certainty is the source of our hope, which we find enshrined in all the invocations of the Our Father. When we need help, Jesus does not tell us to deal with it and go it alone, but to turn to the Father and ask him with trust. All of our needs, from the most obvious and everyday ones like food, health, and work, to that of being forgiven and sustained in temptation, are not the mirror image of our solitude. Instead, there is a Father who always looks at us with love, and who certainly does not abandon us.

Now I have a proposal for you: every one of us has many problems and many needs. Let us think a bit, in silence, about these problems and these needs. Let us also think about the Father, about our Father, who cannot be without us, and who is looking at us in this moment. And all together, with trust and hope, let us pray, "Our Father, who art in heaven . . ."

But Deliver Us
from Evil

*The wheat and the weeds must ripen together
until the time of the harvest. It is forbidden to
jump ahead of the time of reaping! Only then will
the weeds be burned.*

*The Our Father concludes with, "But deliver
us from evil." And at the juvenile prison on the
island of Nisida, across from Naples, one young*

man gave me the gift of a touching confidence.
"There is only one thing I repeat under the covers
before I go to sleep at night: 'Lord, deliver me from
evil.'" Hearing a sixteen-year-old say this made
me aware of the real concreteness of evil. In your
teachings, many times you talk about Satan and
unmask him.

There is evil. Evil is not something intangible
that spreads like the fog of Milan. Evil is
a person, Satan, who is very cunning. The
Lord tells us that when Satan is driven out
he goes away, but after a certain time, when
one is distracted, perhaps after several years,
he comes back worse than before. He does
not stage a home invasion. No, Satan is very
courteous; he knocks at the door, rings, and
enters with his typical seductions and his
companions. In the end, this is the meaning
of the verse "deliver us from evil." We must
be sly, in the good sense of the word, be

sharp, have the ability to discern the lies of
Satan—with whom I am convinced there is
no dialoguing. How did Jesus act with Satan?
He drove him away, or, as he did in the desert,
he used the Word of God. Not even Jesus
ever began a dialogue with Satan, because if
we start to dialogue with him we are lost. He
is more intelligent than we humans are. He
turns us upside down and makes our head
spin. In the end we must say, "Be gone, be
gone!"

*I got excited once when I read a passage in which
you cited a great poet, Léon Bloy: "He who does
not pray to God—"*

"—prays to Satan."

*There is no alternative. And therefore you say that
Evil should rightly be written in upper case, that
"it has a name."*

That is exactly right.

It can even infiltrate our own home?

Yes. However, Satan is astute and pretends to be courteous with us. With us priests, us bishops, he enters with delicacy, but things end up badly if we do not realize it in time.

The Weeds Amid the
Good Wheat

The parable of the wheat and the weeds
confronts the problem of evil in the world
and brings God's patience into focus (cf. Mt
13:24–30, 36–43). The scene unfolds in a
field where the master sows wheat, but one
night the enemy comes and sows weeds, the
term for which in Hebrew comes from the
same root as the name Satan, and recalls the
concept of division. We all know that the

devil is "nettlesome," the one who always
tries to divide persons, families, nations, and
peoples. The servants would like to pull up the
weeds right away, but the master stops them,
with this explanation: "Lest in gathering
the weeds you root up the wheat along with
them" (Mt 13:29). Because we all know that
the weeds, while they are growing, look a lot
like the good wheat, and there is the danger of
confusing the two.

The parable has a twofold teaching. In the
first place, it says that the evil in the world
does not come from God, but from his enemy,
the Fiend. It is curious, the Fiend goes out
at night to sow the weeds, in darkness, in
confusion; he goes where there is no light
to sow the weeds. This enemy is astute. He
has sown evil in the midst of good, so that
it is impossible for us men to separate them

properly; but God, in the end, will be able to do so.

And here we come to the second theme: the contrast between the impatience of the servants and the patient waiting of the field's owner, who represents God. At times we are in a big hurry to judge, classify, put the good over here, the bad over there. . . . But remember the prayer of that arrogant man: "O God, I thank you because I am good; I am not like other men, wicked . . ." (cf. Lk 18:11–12). God, instead, knows how to wait. He looks at the "field" of each person's life with patience and mercy. He sees much better than we do the filth and the evil, but he also sees the sprouts of goodness and waits with assurance for them to mature. God is patient. He knows how to wait. How beautiful this is. Our God is a patient Father, who always waits for us and waits for us with his heart on his sleeve to welcome us, to forgive us. He always forgives us if we go to him.

The master's attitude is that of hope based on the certainty that evil has neither the first nor the last word. And it is thanks to this patient hope of God that the weeds themselves, meaning the evil heart with its many sins, can become good wheat in the end. But be careful. Evangelical patience is not indifference to evil. There must be no confusion between good and evil! In the face of the weeds present in the world, the disciple of the Lord is called to imitate God's patience, to foster hope with the support of an unshakeable trust in the final victory of the good, meaning God.

In the end, in fact, evil will be removed and eliminated. At the time of the harvest, meaning the judgment, the reapers will carry out the master's orders, separating the weeds in order to burn them (cf. Mt 13:30). On that day of the final harvest the judge will be Jesus, he who sowed the good wheat in the world and himself became a "grain of wheat," died and rose again. In the end, we will all be judged with the same measure with which we have judged. The mercy that we have shown to others will be shown to us as well. Let us ask the Blessed Lady, our Mother, to help us grow in patience, in hope, and in mercy with all our brothers.

The Lord's Prayer

We have come to the end of this beautiful prayer,
the most beautiful of all. As Simone Weil noted,
there may never have been another prayer written
that was not already contained in the Pater. To
close the circle, I confess that when I celebrate the
Eucharist I am always amazed by those timorous
words that the priest always speaks before
intoning the prayer: "Obedient to the word of the
Lord and instructed by his divine teaching, we

*dare to say." That "we dare to say" is wonderful,
almost on tiptoe, in hushed tones. It is as if only
together could we find the courage to say "Father."
Christianity cannot exist in solitude.*

We do need courage to pray the Our Father.
We need courage. What I say is this: we must
humble ourselves into saying "Daddy" and to
truly believing that God is the Father who
accompanies us, forgives us, gives us bread,
is attentive to all that we ask, clothes us even
better than the flowers of the field. To believe
is a big risk. We fear. *What if this all is not true?*
To dare, to dare, but we must do this together.
This is why praying together is so beautiful,
because we help one another to dare.

*In fact, as you said in a catechesis when speaking
of the figure of Moses, to pray is to negotiate with
God. If I am together with the people, then I find
the courage to bargain with God, to say to him,*

"Please, calm down, look us in the face; it is true, we are unfaithful, but we are your people." Prayer is sometimes like negotiation.

Abraham negotiated with God when he was about to destroy Sodom and Gomorrah (cf. Gen 18:22–32). Abraham interceded for the just persons of the city, bargaining and negotiating with God, and God replied that he would not destroy it if he could find thirty, twenty-five, twenty, ten just persons in the city.

One would have been enough for God, like a beggar, to enter into that city with his salvation. Yet that day there was not even one just person. . . .

. . .

Pope Francis, thank you for telling us, as pope, about the Our Father. Who taught you the Our Father, when you were little?

My grandmother. My grandmother.

And does it happen to you, at some time during the day, that you just find yourself praying the Our Father without being intentional in your prayer?

No, not without realizing it. I am fortunate that when I set out to pray it comes immediately.

To conclude our encounter I offer you as a gift—seeing that I possess nothing other than the odor of my sheep, of the flock—a verse of Goethe: "What you have inherited from your fathers, you must earn again to make it your own." For us the Our Father is an inheritance. However, it is not enough to inherit it; I must earn it to be able to truly call it my own.

This is why it is important to return to our roots. Above all, in this rootless society, we must return to our roots, earn them again.

Our Father

*We must turn around and feel that there is a
Father who is waiting for us.*

This is why I like to talk so much about
the dialogue between young people and
grandparents, because that is exactly what this
means: return to one's roots.

Let's recite the Our Father together.

> Our Father, who art in heaven,
> hallowed be thy name.
> Thy kingdom come, thy will be done,
> on earth as it is in heaven.
> Give us this day our daily bread,
> and forgive us our trespasses
> as we forgive those who trespass against us.
> And lead us not into temptation,
> but deliver us from evil.

The Prayer of Grandparents Is a Treasure

The lives of the elderly and of grandparents are prayers. They are a gift for the Church. They are a treasure! The elderly, grandmothers, and grandfathers are a great injection of wisdom for society as a whole, especially for people who are too busy, too caught up, too distracted. Let us sing to them. Sing the signs of God, proclaim the signs of God, and pray for them! Let us look to Benedict XVI, who has chosen to spend the last portion of his life in prayer and in listening to God! This is beautiful! A great believer of the past century, of the Orthodox tradition, Olivier Clément, once said, "A civilization in which there is no more prayer is a civilization in which old age no longer has meaning. And this is terrifying, we need first of all elderly who pray, because old age is given to us for this." We need elderly who pray because old age is given to us for this. It is a beautiful thing, the prayer of the elderly.

We can *thank* the Lord for the benefits we have received, and fill up the void of ingratitude that surrounds him. We can *intercede* for the expectations of the new generations, and give dignity to the memory and sacrifices of those who have passed. We can remind ambitious young people that a life without love is a life of desolation. We can tell fearful young people that anguish about the future can be overcome. We can teach young people in love with themselves that there is more joy in giving than in receiving. Grandfathers and grandmothers make up the permanent "choir" of a great spiritual shrine, where the prayer of supplication and the song of praise sustain the community that works and struggles in the field of life.

Prayer, finally, *incessantly purifies the heart*. Praise and supplication to God keep the heart from becoming hardened by resentment and selfishness. How ugly is the cynicism of an elderly person who has lost the sense of his witness, despises young people, and communicates no wisdom about life! And how beautiful instead is the encouragement that the elderly person is able to transmit to the young person seeking the meaning of faith and of life! This is truly the mission of grandparents, the vocation of the elderly. The words of grandparents hold something special for young people. And they know it. I still keep with me, always in my breviary, the words that my grandmother gave to me in writing on the day of my ordination. I read them often, and they do me good.

How I would like to see a Church that challenges the culture of the disposable with the overflowing joy of a new embrace between the young and the old! And this is what I am asking of the Lord today, this embrace!

Afterword

An Our Father Among
the Imprisoned

by Marco Pozza

I left the prison in Padua with just a handful
of words, those of the Pater. The hell of the
penitentiary is our territory on the edge of
despair; the smile of Pope Francis is our
consolation. When the train slows down, the
Eternal City welcomes me with a piece of
graffiti scrawled on a viaduct wall, "Without
the foundation, forget about the heights."

On August 4, 2017, I interviewed Pope
Francis for a television broadcast on the Our
Father. When the elevator opens at Santa
Marta, the pope is already there. No joy
gladdens the heart more than seeing that
someone has been there waiting. "Sit down
here," the pope says. "Take off your jacket, it's
hot today."

I tell him about myself, about the prisoners
I minister to: Enrico, Marzio, the burglars
and thieves. Into that oculus of Santa Marta
I bring him the silent emotion, the affection,
the smiles and laughter of my jailhouse cast
of characters. I spill out for him, like a son to
his father, my whole story. He, with a placid
expression, follows along and encourages me:
"There is no greater grace than shame for one's
sins, Father Marco."

On the pope's table are some of my letters to

him. I see that he has been making notes on them, and I silently rejoice at how the words of an ordinary priest can stand side by side with the prophetic markings of a pope.

"Let's go," he says to me. "It's almost five, and they're waiting for us downstairs. What format should we use for our conversation on the Our Father?"

A daring idea occurs to me: to leave our notes where they are and improvise.

He smiles. It is the smile of a father, full of authenticity, like bread. When we sit down to talk I realize that we are already well on our way. His being a father to me has put me in the best frame of mind to talk about our Father.

At the end of the interview, Pope Francis

handed me a gift. "Take this home with you.
Pray with it when you are troubled." It is a
plaster figurine of a sleeping Saint Joseph.
This is his favorite image of the carpenter who,
alone of all people, can boast that he had God
as his shop boy. That he was father to Christ.

A prison chaplain. The mendicant pope.
Joseph asleep. The next morning God would
haul me back to prison. I would go in armed
with words. A handful of private messages
to share: Franciscan words, disclosures of the
pope, of Papa.

One of the men I minister to in prison is
Enrico. He is made of the kind of cloth that
is rough and paper-thin. For whole seasons, I
have seen him through the jagged frames of
his iron bars. "I've made myself a collection
of all the crimes in the book," he told me.
Evil makes man the subject of jurisprudence.

So many locked up for theft, armed robbery,
trafficking in stolen goods, drug trafficking,
murder, counterfeiting, abuse, terrorism.

The worst, for men, is a crime that is
not found anywhere in the statutes:
misappropriation of paternity. "Nothing hurts
worse than having made my son an orphan,
stripping away his right to grow up with his
father," Enrico tells me. "When he was born
I was already in jail. I have seen my son grow
up from the visiting rooms of the prisons. He
has done a whole triathlon in the prisons: first,
he crawled, then he walked, finally he ran.
One day he ran so fast in the prison that he
got away. He hasn't been able to come see me
since."

Enrico keeps his eyes wide open. He sees
everything clearly. He is a soul in pain looking
out over hell. "When I call my son, I'm

shaking. I already know what he is going to ask me: 'Daddy, when are you coming home?' Receiving my sentence did not bother me, but that question from my son is like the blade of a guillotine and I wait for it to fall through many sleepless nights. Never as a thief did I shed any blood, but I have stolen my child's daddy away. I robbed myself of my own son."

He continues: "Do you want a brief summary of my life? It is easy. I smeared the good name of my father. My father was a good soul, an honest farmer in the Venetian countryside. As for me, by the age of sixteen I had already found a way to make a name for myself: banks, jewelry stores, post offices, arrest, and prison. The first time I came back, he said to me, 'The door is open if you follow the rules.' One year later, in jail again. He closed the door. For good."

In many places, it is a law of necessity that fathers write the rules, and mothers take care of forgiveness. "When my mother was dying," said Enrico, "the police took me to say goodbye to her. 'Remember that I loved you so much,' she whispered to me. When I say 'Mama,' it makes me dizzy."

Give heaven a crack, and it will tear down a fortress. The pope and I shared those words of the poet: "In the cracks is God, who lies in wait." There are many doors in life— automatic, manual, sliding, doors of iron, of bronze, of copper. For a thief, it is a joke to find doors of mercy. Yet that is what God offers, mercy. Mercy in torrents. This was the announcement of the pontiff.

"When I was young, I espoused the will of evil," said Enrico. "Last year I was under attack from evil: cancer. Even prison did not

want me then. I was thrown out. 'Get your
treatment, then you're coming back to prison.'
I was afraid. Where do I go to die? I had
burned all my bridges. *But* a priest flung open
for me the doors of his house. I was used to
being the one who cracked open doors! After
thirty years in prison, if I survive cancer, it
will be because of that door the priest opened
for me, smack-dab in the Year of Mercy,
almost a joke. In front of that door, my
old kingdom died once and for all. His
will won."

One of many ideas lit up the room during my
interview with the pope: the true protagonist
of history is the beggar. I understand that the
features of the mendicant are also those of the
God the poor love, pray to, find new again
every day beside him, find the unexpected, the
unexpectable. The proclamation of God, the

most stunning ever to have come from heaven,
is always the same: that eternity has decided to
confine itself within time. That time has gone
to dwell in eternity in Jesus.

God the mendicant. God the powerful in
powerlessness. God curled up in the squalid
odor of the prison. "To beg" is a verb of
poverty; the daily grind of the poor, the
woman hunched beneath the porticos of the
city, the man rummaging in the garbage, the
prisoner behind bars. The barges, the walls,
the unemployed life, seen up close. Looking
at Jesus, it is true that the God of Francis is
a mendicant of whom we need to take note.
"He had no form or comeliness that we should
look at him." Suffering, miserable to look at,
"as one from whom men hide their faces he
was despised, and we esteemed him not" (Is
53:2, 3). This is the language of Francis. God
is the God of surprises, of the gaps, the God

in ambush, the one adored, meditated upon, eaten. The God who is understood only by conjugating verbs in the passive voice, which is the active form of heavenly grace, letting oneself be surprised, accepting to be loved. Letting God take care of us. Admitting that only God can rejuvenate us from within, "Behold, I make all things new" (Rev 21:5).

God dwells in the poor. "No cell is far enough to keep God out." Francis proclaims to the imprisoned: Mercy! "May the gesture of directing their thought and prayer to the Father each time they cross the threshold of their cell signify for them their passage through the Holy Door." Freedom behind bars, a guarantee of safety. I belong, and I become ever more proud of this, to the humble lineage of the mendicant, whose only treasure is poverty.

The pope as a pilgrim in Bozzolo, in Barbiana at the tomb of the prior, washing feet in the prisons infested with sinners. The pope who enters Lampedusa by boat, who crosses the threshold of the house of a group of married priests. The mendicant pope, postman of a mendicant God. Recognizing God in civilian clothes, in rags, means salvation. We then recognize ourselves better. If we have never trained for his invasion, at least let us be found with sandals on our feet (cf. Ex 12:11). The promise is to be there, regardless of times and circumstances. Love asks for the luxury of having its own way.

Huddled over books in a corner in jail, Marzio looks like he is of no use to anyone. Other prisoners greet him as one greets a survivor. What Marzio remembers of his time in jail is the taste of bread: "In prison, among the discarded, I rediscovered the solidarity that I had seen die on the outside. Inside, sharing the little we had, everyone felt less poor. One does not cook alone. It takes two burners to boil the water, and another to make the sauce. Each prisoner has one burner. It takes three to make good pasta! Food is friendship. For Christmas and Easter, the cooking begins days ahead of time. It is nostalgia: 'The sauce is like my mother's. The ragù like my grandma used to make. The anchovies like those of my seaside home.' Those who break bread together also help to keep each other entertained. Here on the inside the hours never go by. The sounds are always the same: stifled laughter, creaking springs, muffled words. Cries of seagulls, blasphemies, yelling, and code-speak: 'Air, shower, conversation. Magistrate, director, school.'"

To Mass! "As many times as that Bread looked at me, I looked at it. It literally saved me from despair, from feeling that I was damned. I thought we were at the end of the line in there. Now I understand that I was on the launch pad." In prison, every fifteen minutes equals years of aging. Heaven, when the fruit is ripe, endures the wait: "Today you will be with me in Paradise" (Lk 23:43). Today is the completion of the present moment.

"During the years I was in prison, I paid the loss of fatherhood twice over. My father died, and I too died as a father. I saw the family I had built fall apart. Out of too much shame, maybe. 'The wife of a bandit, the daughters of a convict.' The innocents of my home ended up in the floodlights of the town. I ask for forgiveness and then some. I started myself, giving back the forgiveness I received in

prison. I have been forgiven; I have forgiven
the abandonment." A ray of light cast in the
darkness of prison. "It was a debt. There will
come an answer in return, or perhaps not.
There are debts that are turned into credits;
others remain unresolved. I have given
without making any demands. This is what
seemed right to me."

Marzio has more than two thousand prison
nights in his memory. "At first it seemed
that I was being suffocated, that the crater of
cement swallowed me up. It is a receptacle of
evil, a bottomless pit. Temptation is seductive.
It reassures. I had ended up in the land of
temptations; the most deadly was that of no
longer being able to value life. To give up,
to drift, be lazy, do nothing, be a slugabed."
Temptation is a drunkard two steps from the
abyss. When it collapses, heaven ridicules

it. "O death, where is thy victory? O death, where is thy sting?" (1 Cor 15:55). Paul's words are also those of Marzio: "My best temptation has been the temptation to change. Evil has tried to take my life. It has been a temptation. Now I admit that. When one is in hell, the most gigantic temptation is to merit heaven." The vagabond has returned to his town. "After getting out of prison, to the world I am still the crime I committed; I have not yet become a person again. Amen! I will try not to lose sight of God's priorities." When the outrage is gone, God will think of the outcast.

It is a game played with joy, the kind of joy that makes Enrico burst out laughing like a mischievous child. "Deliver me from evil? Look at what a trick he has played on me. I, a thief, would never have thought that the day would come when they would cheat me like this, with a door thrown wide open. Why so much love for an old bandit like me? Now so many things have changed, delivered from evil, why would I care about being one of the bad guys?" Enrico is on the getaway.

I leave the prison. The bells of the nearby church are tolling four: Mass is beginning. Yesterday, in St. Peter's Square, the bells were tolling four. I passed through a gate going into the Vatican; now I pass through a gate going out of prison. Francis, when he looks up, contemplates his basilica, where Michelangelo caressed marble and carved the Mary in the moment of the *Pietà*. I looked up at the pope yesterday and I studied the features of a man who, impelled by the Spirit, touched the doors of prison cells and turned them into holy doors.

Our Father

I think of Marzio, a few kilometers away. I imagine Enrico making dinner for his priests. I think of the Pater Noster.

We have discovered unknown interior spaces, which are still waiting to be explored. Poor Christs have made a comeback: they act as sentinels of mercy.

Sources

Fr. Marco Pozza's interview with Pope Francis was conducted at Santa Marta on August 4, 2017, for TV2000, Italy.

The preface, "Pray to the Father," reproduces, in part, with variations and additions, the homily at Santa Marta on June 20, 2013, published with the title "We Cannot Pray to the Father If We Have Enemies in Our

Hearts," in Pope Francis, *The Truth Is an Encounter*, Rizzoli 2014.

"I Will Not Leave You Orphans"
    General audience, January 28, 2015

Fathers and the Our Father
    General audience, February 4, 2015

Participating with Prayer in the Work of Salvation
    Angelus, July 24, 2016

The Kingdom of God Needs Our Participation
    Angelus, June 14, 2015

Mary's Total "Yes" to the Will of God
    Angelus, December 8, 2016

Sources

Feed the Hungry
General audience, October 19, 2016

Training for Giving and for Forgiveness
General audience, November 4, 2015

The Foundation of Our Hope
General audience, June 7, 2017

The Weeds Amid the Good Wheat
Angelus, July 20, 2014

The Prayer of Grandparents Is a Treasure
General audience, March 11, 2015